Anonymus

The dawn of day

First prayers and meditations for the young

Anonymus

The dawn of day
First prayers and meditations for the young

ISBN/EAN: 9783741179105

Manufactured in Europe, USA, Canada, Australia, Japa

Cover: Foto ©Lupo / pixelio.de

Manufactured and distributed by brebook publishing software (www.brebook.com)

Anonymus

The dawn of day

Mater dolorosa.

The Dawn of Day:

FIRST PRAYERS AND MEDITATIONS

FOR THE YOUNG.

Compiled from Approved Sources.

LONDON:
BURNS & LAMBERT, 17 PORTMAN STREET,
AND 63 PATERNOSTER ROW.

CONTENTS.

	PAGE
Morning Prayers	1
Night Prayers	3
Child's Prayer for a Sick Person	3
Prayer to be said by a Sick Child	4
Hymn	5
Prayer for Children when they cannot go to sleep	6
Hymn	7
Examination of Conscience	8
Prayer after the Examen	9
Prayers for Mass	10
Gospel of St. John	30
Prayer after Mass	32
First Meditation: Introductory	33
Second Meditation: On Filial Piety	39
Third Meditation: On Meekness and Docility	41
Fourth Meditation: On Brotherly Love	44
Fifth Meditation: On the Love of our Neighbour	48
Sixth Meditation: On Truth	52
Seventh Meditation: On Pride	56
Eighth Meditation: On Temperance	61
Ninth Meditation: On Diligence	64
Last Meditation: On Temptation	68
Vespers	73

PRAYERS FOR A CHILD.

MORNING PRAYERS.

✠ In the name of the Father, and of the Son, and of the Holy Ghost. Amen.

My God and Father, who art in heaven, I love thee, and I thank thee for having given me life. Give me grace to obey my parents, and all those who take care of me. Bless me, O my God, and bless also [my father and mother, my grandfather and grandmother, my brothers and sisters, my relations and friends, my nurse,*] and all the persons who live in this house. Give us all that is needful for our souls and bodies. Keep sickness far from us, and grant to our country peace and plenty. I pray also, O my God, for the people of other countries, who are our brethren, since they too are thy children. Amen.

* This will of course be varied according to circumstances.

Our Father, who art in heaven, hallowed be thy name: thy kingdom come; thy will be done on earth as it is in heaven. Give us this day our daily bread: and forgive us our trespasses, as we forgive them that trespass against us. And lead us not into temptation; but deliver us from evil. Amen.

Hail, Mary, full of grace; the Lord is with thee: blessed art thou among women, and blessed is the fruit of thy womb, Jesus. Holy Mary, Mother of God, pray for us sinners now, and at the hour of our death. Amen.

Angel of God, sent from heaven to take care of me, guard, direct, and govern me throughout this day, and every day of my life.

Dear Infant Jesus, have mercy on me.

Sweet Mother of Jesus, be a mother to me.

Holy St. Joseph, pray for me.

May the souls of the faithful departed rest in peace.

✠ In the name of the Father, and of the Son, and of the Holy Ghost. Amen.

NIGHT PRAYERS.

My God, I thank thee for having preserved me during this day; I beg thee to pardon all that I have done wrong, and to give me grace to do better to-morrow. Bless [my father and mother, brothers and sisters, and all my relations, my nurse,] and all who are in this house; and grant that thy holy angels may overshadow us with their wings, and give us sweet sleep; and may we all wake to-morrow morning strengthened by rest, that we may be able to rise diligently to praise and serve thee. Amen.

Our Father. Hail, Mary. Angel of God. Sweet Infant Jesus, &c. May the souls, &c. ✠ In the name, &c.

Child's Prayer for a Sick Person.

O my God, I believe that thou canst do any thing that thou pleasest, and that nothing is impossible or difficult to thee. I beseech thee, heal ―― of his (*or* her) grievous sickness, and take away the pain he (*or* she) is suffering. But if it is not thy will to give him health, I pray thee to give him patience in his sufferings, and to grant all of us submission to thy holy will. Amen.

St. Raphael, physician of souls, consoler of all in trouble, pray for ———.

Our Father. Hail, Mary. May the souls, &c.

Prayer to be said by a Sick Child.

Dear Jesus, lover of little children, have pity on me, a poor sick child. Make me, O Lord, patient and meek, and give me grace to obey those who nurse me. Bless the medicine they bring to cure me, and give me courage to bear with patience all the pain that thou dost require me to suffer for the good of my soul. Amen.

Holy Archangel St. Raphael, physician of souls, helper of all who are sick and weak, pray for me.

My dear angel guardian, watch over me, pray for me, and make me love thee, and think of thee both by night and by day.

Hymn.

Jesu, brightness of the Father!
    Life and strength of all who live,
In the presence of the angels
    Glory to thy name we give.
And thy wondrous praise rehearse,*
Singing in alternate† verse.

Hail, too, ye angelic powers!
    Hail, ye thrones celestial!
Hail, Physician of Salvation,
    Guide of life, blest Raphael,
Who the foe of all mankind
Didst in links of iron bind.

Oh, may Christ be our protection;
    Shelter us from harm this day;
Keep us pure and free from sin;
    Save us from the enemy;
And vouchsafe us, of his grace,
In his Paradise a place,

---

* The word "rehearse," as it is used here, means to repeat, to recite, to sing, or say out loud, as we say Vespers.

† "Alternate" means by turns. You will have noticed at Vespers that one verse of a psalm is said by one set of people, and the next verse by others.

Glory to the Almighty Father,
   Sing we now in anthems sweet;
Glory to the great Redeemer,
   Glory to the Paraclete:
Three in One, and One in Three,
Throughout all eternity.

Prayer for Children when they cannot go to sleep.

O great Creator of all things, I know that thou hast given us the day for work, and the night for rest, and that the darkness is sent to make thy creatures go to sleep. I pray thee take from me all foolish fears, and let sweet sleep close my eyes. In heaven all is light, and the holy angels are singing thy praises, and bowing down before thy throne. Thou art there, brighter than the sun, and on thy right hand stands Blessed Mary, my sweet Mother, shining with glory, and all the Saints are there crowned with stars. I can see nothing but darkness round me, but I know that it is bright in heaven; and I pray thee, O Father of Light, to let thy beautiful angels keep watch round my bed, and give rest to my eyelids, and peace to my soul. Amen.

Hymn.

Light of the soul, O Saviour blest !
Soon as thy presence fills the breast,
Darkness and guilt are put to flight,
And all is sweetness and delight.

Pure Light of Light ! eternal day,
Who dost the Father's brightness share ;
Our chant the midnight silence breaks ;
Be nigh, and hearken to our prayer.

Examination of Conscience.

1. Have you said your prayers this morning?
2. Have you tried to keep still while you were saying your prayers?
3. Have you tried not to look about?
4. Have you tried to pay attention, and not to let yourself think of any thing but Almighty God while you were at prayers?
5. Have you been obedient to your parents, and those appointed to take care of you?
6. Have you been good and docile with your nurse?
7. Have you paid great attention while learning your Catechism?
8. Have you tried to understand and remember all that your teachers have said to you?
9. Have you spoken the truth all day long?
10. Have you been kind to your brothers and sisters, or your companions?
11. Have you tried not to be passionate or sulky?
12. Have you taken care not to tell tales, or complain of your brothers and sisters, or companions?
13. Have you tried not to be greedy?

EXAMINATION OF CONSCIENCE.

14. Have you remembered not to ask at dinner for any thing, but taken what was given you contentedly?

15. Have you cried when something you wanted has been refused you?

16. Have you been angry because something you liked was given to one of your companions?

17. Have you thought of the poor, and wished to give them something?

18. Have you been kind to the servants, and tried not to give them more trouble than is necessary?

19. Have you taken care to speak kindly and gently to every body?

20. Have you been tender and kind to animals?

21. Have you tried not to tear your clothes and your books? not to break or lose your toys? not to hurt, waste, or destroy any thing in the house?

[This can be shortened for a very little child.]

Prayer after the Examen.

O my God, I ask pardon for all my faults. I am very sorry for them, because sin is displeasing to thee, my kind Heavenly Father. I will try to-morrow not to do the wrong things I have done to-day. I beg of thee to give me grace to correct my faults, and to make myself good and reasonable. Amen.

Sweet Virgin Mary, Mother of Jesus, help me to be good, and pray to your dear Son to forgive all I have done wrong.

My dear angel guardian, pray for me.

PRAYERS FOR MASS.

Before Mass begins, say to yourself,

I am going to hear Mass. I must be very attentive, because Mass is a most solemn thing. The priest is going to offer sacrifice, and all the angels and saints in heaven will look down with reverence and joy, and watch all that is done in this church. They will love me if I pay attention, and recollect how beautiful and solemn a thing the Holy Sacrifice of the Mass is. Jesus is coming. I must think of him, and not look about, or let myself get tired. Sweet Infant Jesus, make me think of you, and make me love you more and more every time I hear Mass.

Sweet Virgin Mary, pray for me to the dear Infant Jesus, and give me good thoughts.

My own dear angel, stay close to me. I wish I could see you kneeling by my side, and touch your beautiful soft wings.

But though I cannot see you, I know you are there. Pray for me, and offer this Mass for me, and keep foolish and bad thoughts from coming into my head, and make my heart pleasing to Jesus, so that I may profit by the Mass I am going to hear.

When you see the priest coming in, put yourself on your knees, and watch for the moment when he begins Mass. He will stand at the foot of the altar, and make the sign of the cross. Then do you, too, sign yourself with the cross, saying,

In the name of the Father, and of the Son, and of the Holy Ghost. Amen.

And pray thus:

Prayer at the beginning of Mass.

I adore thee, O my God; and I firmly believe that the Mass I am going to hear is the sacrifice of the Body and Blood of thy Son Jesus Christ, my Saviour. Oh, grant that I may assist at it with the awe due to so holy a mystery; and grant that by the merits of the Victim there offered for me, I myself may become an agreeable sacrifice to thee, who livest and reignest, One God, world without end. Amen.

The Confiteor.

I confess to Almighty God, to blessed Mary ever Virgin, to blessed Michael the

Archangel, to blessed John the Baptist, to the holy Apostles Peter and Paul, and to all the saints, that I have sinned exceedingly, in thought, word, and deed, through my fault, through my fault, through my most grievous fault. Therefore I beseech the blessed Mary ever Virgin, blessed Michael the Archangel, blessed John the Baptist, the holy Apostles Peter and Paul, and all the saints, to pray to the Lord our God for me. May Almighty God have mercy on me, forgive me my sins, and bring me to everlasting life. Amen. May the almighty and merciful Lord grant me ✠ pardon, absolution, and remission of all my sins. Amen.

After the "Confiteor," the priest goes up to the altar, saying,

Take away from us, we beseech thee, our iniquities, that we may be worthy to enter with pure minds into the holy of holies, through Christ our Lord. Amen.

Say the same with him, and when he kisses the altar, say,

Dear Lord Jesus, I love thee with my whole heart; I wish I could kiss thy sacred feet.

When the priest is come up to the altar, he goes to the book, and reads the "Introit," or En-

trance of the Mass, which is generally a sentence taken out of the Scripture. You can say this:

O my God, direct my steps in the way of thy commandments, and grant that nothing may ever separate me from thy love.

Blessed are they that are undefiled in the way, that walk in the law of the Lord.

Glory be to the Father, and to the Son, and to the Holy Ghost; as it was in the beginning, is now, and ever shall be, world without end. Amen.

The priest returns to the middle of the altar, and says with the clerk "Kyrie eleison," or "Lord have mercy on us," which is said three times in honour of the Blessed Trinity. After the "Kyrie," he says the "Gloria in excelsis," which begins with the very words the angels sung at Bethlehem when they appeared to the shepherds on Christmas night.

Glory to God on high, and on earth peace to men of good will. We praise thee; we bless thee; we adore thee; we glorify thee; we give thee thanks for thy great glory, O Lord God, heavenly King, God the Father Almighty. O Lord Jesus Christ, the only-begotten Son; O Lord God, Lamb of God, Son of the Father, thou who takest away the sins of the world, have mercy on us; thou who takest away the sins of the world, receive our prayers; thou who sittest at the right hand of the Father, have mercy on us. For thou only art holy; thou only art the Lord; thou only, O Jesus Christ, with the Holy Ghost, art most high in the glory of God the Father. Amen.

This, being a hymn of joy, is left out in Masses for the Dead, and in the Masses of the Sundays of Advent and Lent. At High Mass the priests and the congregation sit down while the "Gloria" is sung. At the end of the "Gloria," the priest kisses the altar, and turning to the people, says,

Dominus vobiscum.
The Lord be with you.

As often as this salutation is repeated, pray that our Lord may be always with you, with his ministers, and with his people.

The priest then says,

Oremus,
Let us pray;

and reads the Collects, or prayers of the day, ending them with the words "per Dominum nostrum," &c. (through our Lord Jesus Christ, &c.).

Prayer at the Collects.

O Almighty and Eternal God, we humbly beseech thee mercifully hear the prayers offered thee by thy servant in the name of thy whole Church, and in behalf of us thy people. Accept them to the honour of thy name, and the good of our souls; and grant us all mercy, grace, and salvation, through our Lord Jesus Christ. Amen.

After the Collects, the priest reads the Epistle. At the end of it you will hear the clerk answer,

Deo gratias.
Thanks be to God.

This is said to express our thankfulness for the heavenly doctrine read to us in the Epistle.

Prayer at the Epistle.

O my God, I thank thee that thou hast called me to the knowledge of thy holy law. I desire to receive with all my heart thy divine commandments, and to hear with attention and reverence what thou sayest to us by the mouths of thy prophets and apostles.

Give me grace, O my God, not only to know thy will, but also to do it.

Then follow some sentences called the "Gradual," which are different every day. After the "Gradual," the book is removed to the other side of the altar, which is called the Gospel side. The priest, before he reads the Gospel, stands a short time bowing down before the middle of the altar; begging of God to cleanse his heart and his lips, that he may be worthy to declare those heavenly words.

At the beginning of the Gospel, the priest says,

Dominus vobiscum.
The Lord be with you.

and then tells out of which of the evangelists the Gospel is taken, saying, "Sequentia S. Evangelii secundum," &c.; that is,"What follows is of the holy Gospel according to St. —," &c. At these words, both priest and people make the sign of the cross: first upon their foreheads, to signify that they are not ashamed of the cross of Christ; secondly upon their mouths, to signify that they will ever profess it in their words; and thirdly upon their breasts, to signify that they will always keep it in their hearts. The clerk answers,

Gloria tibi Domine.
Glory be to thee, O Lord.

At the Gospel we stand up, to declare our readiness to do whatsoever our Lord commands.

At the Gospel.

O Jesus, thou hast the words of eternal life; teach me, I pray thee, what I must do to gain a place in heaven.

"If thou wilt enter into life, keep the commandments. Thou shalt love the Lord thy God with thy whole heart, and with thy whole soul, and with thy whole mind, and with thy whole strength. Seek first the kingdom of God and his justice, and all other things shall be added unto you. Be perfect, as your Father in heaven is perfect. Love your neighbour as yourself. Love your enemies; do good to them that hate you, and pray for them that persecute you. Happy they who hear the word of God and keep it."

At the end of the Gospel, the clerk answers,
Laus tibi, Christe.
Praise be to thee, O Christ.

And the priest kisses the book, in reverence to those sacred words which he has been reading out of it. Then upon Sundays and many other holy days he recites the

Nicene Creed.

I believe in one God, the Father Almighty, Maker of heaven and earth, and of all things visible and invisible. And in one Lord Jesus Christ, the only-begotten Son of God, born of the Father, before all ages; God of God, Light of Light, true God of true God; begotten, not made; consubstantial to the Father, by whom all things were made. Who for us men, and for our salvation, came down from heaven, and was incarnate by the Holy Ghost of the Virgin Mary, and was made man. [*Here kneel in honour of our Lord's Incarnation.*] He was crucified also for us, suffered under Pontius Pilate, and was buried. The third day he rose again with glory, to judge both the living and the dead; of whose kingdom there shall be no end.

And I believe in the Holy Ghost, the Lord and Giver of life, who proceedeth from the Father and the Son; who, together with the Father and the Son, is adored and glorified; who spake by the prophets. And one holy Catholic and Apostolic Church. I confess one baptism for the remission of sins. And I look for the resurrection of the dead, and the life of the world to come. Amen.

Then the priest turns to the people, and says,
Dominus vobiscum.
The Lord be with you.

And then he reads from the book a sentence of the Scripture, which is called the "Offertory." At the Offertory it is usual to give some money, as an offering for the Church or for the poor. If it tires you to kneel a long time, you can sit down at the Offertory. At the Offertory you will see the priest uncover the chalice, and take in his hand the paten, and offer up the bread to God; then he goes to the corner of the altar, takes the wine, and pours it into the chalice, and mingles with it a little water, in remembrance of the blood and water that issued out of our Saviour's side. After this, he returns to the middle of the altar, and offers up the chalice. When you see the priest uncover the chalice, you can pray thus:

Prayer at the Offertory.

Accept, O eternal Father, this offering, which is here made to thee by thy minister

PRAYERS FOR MASS. 19.

in the name of us all here present, and of thy whole Church. It is as yet only bread and wine; but by a miracle of thy power and grace it will soon be changed into the body and blood of Jesus Christ.

You can add "Our Father," and "Glory be to the Father," if you have time.

Then the priest, bowing down, begs that this sacrifice may find acceptance with God, and blesses the bread and wine with the sign of the cross. You may join with him, and say,

Come, O Almighty and eternal God, the Sanctifier, and bless this Sacrifice prepared for thy holy name.

Then you will see the priest wash his fingers, saying what is called the "Lavabo," during which you can say,

O most pure and holy God, wash my soul, I beseech thee, from every stain; and grant that I may be worthy to assist, with a clean heart, at this most holy sacrifice.

Then you will see the priest bow down at the middle of the altar, and you can say,

O most holy and adorable Trinity, deign to accept this our sacrifice, in memory of our Saviour's passion, resurrection, and glorious ascension. Let those saints, whose memory we celebrate on earth, remember us before thy throne in heaven, and obtain mercy for us through the same Lord Jesus Christ. Amen.

Then the priest will kiss the altar, and turn to the people, and say the

Orate Fratres.

Brethren, pray that my sacrifice and yours may be acceptable to God the Father Almighty.

Say with the clerk:

Receive, O Lord, this sacrifice at the hands of thy priest, to the praise and glory of thine own name, for our benefit, and that of all thy holy Church.

Then the priest says the prayers called "Secreta," which are different every day. You can say:

Mercifully hear our prayers, O Lord, and graciously accept the oblation which we thy servants make to thee through our Lord Jesus Christ. Amen.

Then the priest says aloud, "Per omnia sæcula sæculorum," that is, "World without end." If you have been sitting, you should remember to kneel here.

At the Preface.

Let us lift ourselves up to heaven, O my soul, and give thanks to the Lord our God. The angels in heaven are singing thy praise. May I, great God, unite my heart and voice to their celestial songs, and cry out with them,

Holy, holy, holy, Lord God of Sabaoth. Heaven and earth are full of thy glory. Hosanna in the highest. Blessed is he that cometh in the name of the Lord. Hosanna in the highest.

This last part of the Preface is called the "Sanctus;" and when the priest repeats the word *sanctus*, or holy, three times, the acolyte rings the bell. After the Preface follows the Canon of the Mass, which is the most solemn part of this divine service. Here you should try more than ever to fix your attention; and remember that this is the time to pray for your parents, brothers, and sisters, relations, friends, both living and dead; and you must not forget to pray for our Holy Father Pope Pius IX., for all bishops and priests in all countries, for the bishop of the diocese where you live, and all his priests, and especially for your own pastor, and the priest who is saying Mass, and for the congregation who are hearing Mass with you. You can say "Our Father," "Hail Mary," "Glory be to the Father," and "Eternal rest," offering them up for your own soul, and for all those persons just spoken of, or you may say the following prayers:

Prayer at the Canon.

We humbly pray thee, most merciful Father, through Jesus Christ, thy Son, our Lord, that thou wouldst deign to accept and bless this holy sacrifice which thy priest is offering to thee for thy holy Catholic Church, to which may it please thee to grant peace, as also to perfect, unite, and govern it, throughout the world, together with thy servant Pius our Pope, our Bishop, as also all believers and professors of the Catholic and Apostolic Faith. Be mindful, O Lord, of thy servants,—

Here pray for your friends, and every body you have been taught to pray for. Then think of heaven, and of the Blessed Virgin Mary, Mother of our Lord and God Jesus Christ, and the blessed Apostles and Martyrs, and all the saints; and fancy that they are all looking down on the church where you are hearing Mass, and praying for you, and every one in it. You will hear the bell rung once, when the priest spreads his hands over the oblation. Now the most solemn moment of the Mass is coming. Keep yourself still, shut your eyes, and say to your angel guardian:

O my dear Angel, take care of me now, and ask our Lord to bless me when he comes down from heaven. Speak to him for me because I am a poor weak child, and cannot find words fit to be said at this awful moment.

When the priest pronounces the words of consecration, keep your eyes cast down; and when he kneels to adore the Sacred Host, and then rising, lifts it on high, a bell will be rung three times, and at the sound of this bell every one ought to bow down their heads to adore our Lord Jesus Christ. Say in your heart,

At the Elevation.

Dear Lord Jesus Christ, I adore thee, hiding thyself under the form of bread.

Sweet Sacrament, we thee adore;
Oh, make us love thee more and more.

Or this,

Saviour of the world, save me: for by thy cross and by thy blood thou hast redeemed me: help me, I beseech thee, O my God. Amen.

✠ Then stay quite still, with your head bent down, till you hear the bell rung again, when the priest elevates the chalice, and adores the Blood of our Lord. Do you, too, adore the Precious Blood of Christ, and say,

Hail, Precious Blood of my Saviour! cleanse, sanctify, and preserve my soul, that nothing may ever separate me from thee. Oh, let not this sacrifice be offered for me in vain, but make me, now and for ever, wholly thine. Amen.

Or this,

The Body and Blood of our Lord Jesus Christ profit me, a sinner, as an eternal remedy unto life everlasting. Amen.

Memento for the Dead.

Be mindful, O Lord, of thy servants who are gone before us. Grant to all that rest in Christ a place of refreshment, light, and peace, through the same Christ our Lord. Amen.

Grant, O Lord, that the souls of my relations and friends, and all the souls I ought to pray for, may be refreshed by this Mass. Grant, O Lord, that, when the time comes for me to follow them, I may be prepared to appear before thee; and when I die, let not my soul delay long to enter Paradise.

O my dear Angel, guide and protect me now, and all through my life.

Holy Mary, Mother of God, pray for us sinners now, and at the hour of our death. Amen.

You will see the priest uncover the chalice, kneel down, and rise up again. Then he will take the Host in his right hand, and the chalice in his left, and will sign the sign of the cross three times across the chalice; and then he will kneel again, and rising up, say aloud,

Per omnia sæcula sæculorum.
For ever and ever.

And the acolyte will answer,
Amen.

Say with him "Our Father," and this prayer,

Thy Body was broken, and thy Blood was shed for us; grant that the commemoration of this holy mystery may obtain for us peace, and that those who receive it may find everlasting rest.

Then kneeling down, and rising up again, the priest says,
Agnus Dei.

Say,
Lamb of God, who takest away the sins of the world, have mercy on us.

Lamb of God, who takest away the sins of the world, have mercy on us.

Lamb of God, who takest away the sins of the world, grant us peace.

The priest then says some prayers by way of preparation for receiving the Blessed Sacrament; and then, after kneeling, he rises and says,

I will take the Bread of heaven, and will call upon the name of the Lord.

Then he says the
Domine, non sum dignus, &c.
which means,

Lord, I am not worthy that thou shouldst enter under my roof; say but the word, and my soul shall be healed.

You will hear the bell rung three times here, as a sign that the priest is going to receive the Blessed Sacrament. Bend your head a little, and keep quite still during this solemn part of the Mass. Those persons among the congregation who are to receive communion will go up to the sanctuary after the bell has rung, and kneel down, and wait till the priest opens the door of the tabernacle, and takes out the Pyx or Ciborium, which is a beautiful vessel, where our Lord, under the form of bread, deigns to dwell, in order to be ready to feed his people with the heavenly manna. Recollect that all those persons whom you have seen walking up to the sanctuary, and kneeling down before the altar, are going to be fed with the Bread of Life. Do not look at them in a thoughtless way, and, above all, never allow yourself to stare at them, or to take notice of their dress, their looks, or their manner. You should think to yourself that in a few minutes those persons will have received the Blessed Sacrament; and you must respect them, as you would respect what is holy, for the sake of our Lord, who deigns to enter into them. While the priest is giving them communion, fix your eyes on your book, and say the following prayers:

O most loving Jesus, I pray thee to bless me, and cause me to receive thee spiritually. Come to me, dear Lord, and fill my soul with thy presence, and prepare it for that happy time when I too shall be permitted to approach thy altar, and partake of the heavenly manna. Amen.

Bread of Life, descended from heaven!
Have mercy on us.
Food of Angels! hidden Manna!
Have mercy on us.
Body of Jesus! Lamb of God!
Have mercy on us.

O God, who, under this wonderful Sacrament, hast left us a memorial of thy passion, grant us, we beseech thee, so to venerate the sacred mysteries of thy Body and Blood, that we may ever feel within us the fruit of thy redemption. Amen.

O Godhead hid, devoutly I adore thee,
Who truly art within the forms before me;
To thee my heart I bow with bended knee,
As failing quite in contemplating thee.
Jesu, whom for the present veiled I see,
What I so thirst for, oh, vouchsafe to me,
That I may see thy countenance unfolding,
And may be blest thy glory in beholding.
Jesu, eternal Shepherd, hear our cry,
Increase the faith of all whose souls on thee rely.

If there are a great many communicants, and you find it difficult to keep your attention fixed on your book, shut your eyes, and try to fancy the angels adoring the Blessed Sacrament. Imagine to yourself that hundreds of angels are in the sanctuary, some close to the people who are receiving holy communion, putting good thoughts into their hearts; others attending on the priest; others floating in the air, one above another up to the very roof of the church, all adoring the Blessed Sacrament, and praying for the people who are being fed with angels' food. Think how lovely would be the sight if our eyes were able to see it, and beg the sweet angels to obtain for you a reverent and loving heart, and then say these short prayers:

O sacred Heart of Jesus, I love thee, and desire to love thee more and more. O Heart of Jesus, burning with love of us, kindle in our hearts the love of thee. O sacred Heart of Jesus, mayest thou be known, loved, and adored throughout the whole world! O Heart of my dear Redeemer, may the love of thy friends atone for all the injuries and neglect which thou dost suffer. Sacred Heart of Jesus, have mercy on us.

Immaculate Heart of Mary, pray for us.

After every one has been to communion, the priest goes to the Missal, and reads a sentence called the Communion, after which he turns to the people, saying,

Dominus vobiscum,

The Lord be with you;

and returning to the book, reads the prayers

called the Post Communion. Then he greets the people again with

> Dominus vobiscum,

and tells them to depart with

> Ite missa est;

the clerk answering,

> Deo gratias.
> Thanks be to God.

Then, bowing down before the altar, he makes a short prayer to the Blessed Trinity, and, turning to the people, gives his blessing in the name of the Blessed Trinity. Here we sign ourselves with the sign of the cross, and rise up when the priest crosses to the north side of the altar, to read the beginning of the Gospel of St. John, which is the end of the office. The people stand during this Gospel, till the priest comes to these words,

> Et verbum caro factum est,
> And the Word was made flesh;

when both priests and people kneel down in honour of the Incarnation. The clerk answers,

> Deo gratias.

At the last Prayer.

O my God, I have seen thee offered up for my sake; grant that I may desire to offer myself up for thy glory. I accept willingly all the crosses that it shall please thee to send me. I bless them and receive them from thy hand, and unite them to thine. Make me profit by the holy mysteries I have been allowed to be present at, and grant that this day I may not fall into any sin; and, above all, carefully avoid giving way to those faults which my nature tempts me to the most strongly.

At the last Blessing.

Bless, O Lord, these holy resolutions; bless us all by the hand of thy priest, and may thy blessing rest for ever upon us. ✠ In the name of the Father, and of the Son, and of the Holy Ghost. Amen.

Gospel of St. John.

In the beginning was the Word, and the Word was with God, and the Word was God: the same was in the beginning with God. All things were made by him, and without him was made nothing that was made: in him was life, and the life was the light of men: and the light shineth in darkness, and the darkness did not comprehend it.

There was a man sent from God, whose name was John. This man came for a witness, to give testimony of the light, that all men might believe through him.

He was not the light, but came to give testimony of the light. He was the true light which enlighteneth every man that cometh into this world.

He was in the world, and the world was made by him, and the world knew him not. He came unto his own, and his own received him not. But as many as received him, to them he gave power to become the sons of God: to those that believe in his name, who are born not of blood, nor of the will of the flesh, nor of the will of man, but of God. AND THE WORD WAS MADE FLESH [*here the people kneel down*], and dwelt among us; and we saw his glory, as it were the glory of the Only-begotten of the Father, full of grace and truth.

You can read the Gospel while the priest reads it, or say this prayer:

Divine Word, only Son of the Father, Light of the world, descended from heaven to show us the way thither, let me not be like the faithless Jews who would not believe in thee as their Messiah. Let me not become blind like them; but give me more light day by day, till I come to know thee, and to understand what thou wouldst have me to do. Word made flesh, I adore thee with the deepest reverence; I put my whole trust in thee, hoping firmly that as thou didst come down into this world, and take upon thee the form of an infant to save us all, thou wilt grant to me, thy child, the graces necessary to sanctify myself, and to dwell with thee one day in heaven for ever and ever. Amen.

Prayer after Mass.

I thank thee, O my God, through Jesus Christ thy Son, that thou hast been pleased to deliver him up to death for us, and to give us his body and blood, both as a sacrament and a sacrifice, in these holy mysteries. May all heaven and earth bless and praise thee for all thy mercies! Pardon me, O Lord, all the distractions and negligences which I have been guilty of this day in thy sight, and let me not depart without thy blessing. May all my thoughts, words, and actions tend always to thy glory, through the same Jesus Christ our Lord. Amen.

As you leave the church or chapel, speak in your heart to your angel guardian, and beg him to take care of you all day long, to put good into your mind, and to help you to keep the good resolutions you have made.

MEDITATIONS AND READINGS FOR CHILDREN.

———◆———

FIRST MEDITATION.

Introductory.

THE power of God is infinite. He can do any thing he pleases. He is the creator of all things. It was he who made the blue sky, with the sun to give us light by day, and the moon and stars to shine by night. He made the earth with its green grass and waving trees, the fresh air, the sweet flowers and the cooling fruits. He made the great rivers, the little brooks, and the wide open sea, with all the fishes that swim about in them. He made, too, all the animals that dwell upon the earth: the savage lions and tigers, and the gentle lambs and obedient horses; the birds that fly about in the air singing for joy; the bees that make sweet honey; the little ants that are always at work; the beautiful butterflies that flutter from flower to flower. No man can make any of these things. All we can do is to imitate them, or draw pictures of them. But you know how much better a real flower is than a mock one, and how different a real lamb or a real dog is from one bought at a toy-shop. Men can make images, but they cannot give them life. God alone can breathe the breath of life into the creatures he has formed out of nothing. He is, then, our sovereign Lord and Master, and we ought to fear him, love him, and revere him above all things.

God has not only given us life like unto the life he has bestowed on the animals, but he has also given us a reasonable soul capable of knowing and loving him. You can feel something within you that makes you quite different to a cat or a dog. A dog has a great deal of sense and a most loving heart, but you know he cannot *understand* in the same way that you do. The cleverest dog that ever lived could not learn to read, if you held the letters before his eyes all day long, and tried to make him understand them his whole life through; that is because a dog has no soul. He does God's will without knowing it, just as the plants and trees do God's will according to their nature. The birds sing the praises of their creator; the stars show forth the glory of God; the wind and the rain, the ice and the snow, the sunshine and the storm-cloud, all bless and praise God in the way he has appointed them to do. But we human creatures, who have a soul capable of understanding God, must praise him in a different manner. We must take pains to learn all we can about him; what he requires us to do, and what he wishes us to be.

Our soul has three powers, as you learn in the Catechism: the Will, the Memory, and the Understanding. You know what it is to *understand* any thing. Grown-up people can understand much more than children can, and you can understand more than a baby can: that is because the powers in a baby's soul are not as strong as in yours. A baby has arms and legs, but till it grows older, it cannot use them as you can use yours; and so, though the baby's soul has understanding, it cannot use it as you can use yours. You can understand what it is to choose between good and evil. If you are ill, and you are told that medicine will make you better, the power in your soul which we call Understanding, or Reason, makes you able to believe it; and the other power which we call the Will gives you strength to drink up the bitter draught courageously. A baby cannot understand what is said to it, and therefore, when it is necessary for it to take physic, the medicine must be forced down its poor little throat *against its will.* Now your understanding makes you able to be reasonable, and to choose between the little evil of taking the medicine, and the great evil of going on suffering pain through illness. Just in the same way we all use our reason to choose between small evils or losses and great ones. Suppose, now, I go into the garden on a spring day wishing to make a nosegay of white flowers, and finding none in the beds, I am tempted to gather a quantity of blossoms off a cherry-tree. (Of course, I mean if it is my own garden, or, at least, my own cherry-tree.) Well, I must consider whether I prefer having the flowers now, or the cherries later on; whether I had not better do without the nosegay now, which will be a small loss, than lose the fruit in the summer, which will be a greater one.

God has given us a Divine Book, written by Prophets and Apostles, inspired by the

Holy Ghost. This book is called the Holy Scripture, and when you are old enough to understand it, you will be allowed to read it; that is, if you try to be obedient and good, and show, by paying attention at your prayers, that you really do wish to please Almighty God.

Nothing happens in this world without God's knowing it, and allowing it to happen. Every thing we have is given to us by him. If we are rich, and have good houses to live in, good clothes to wear, plenty of every thing we want, or like to have, it is because God chooses it should be so. Why he makes some rich and others poor, we cannot tell. He knows every thing. He can see all we do when we are quite by ourselves. He can look through us into our hearts, and know what we are thinking about; and so he can judge quite well what is best for every body, and he takes care to give to all his creatures exactly what is most likely to make them think about their souls, and try to go heaven. Therefore we must always put our trust in him; and we need never be afraid in any danger, because we are sure he will always take care of us; nor should we murmur or complain if we are poor, or sick, or have something hard to bear, because troubles are sent to us to make us better, and if we bear them well, God will reward us in heaven. When we love people, we think a great deal about them, and when they are out of our sight, we do not forget them. You know how you feel when your father or your mother is away from home. You count the hours for them to come back, and you run to meet them when you hear them coming. Well, that is the way very good people feel towards God. They often speak to him in their hearts, and say, "O my God, I love thee, but teach me to love thee more and more." And they like going to church, and praying in their own rooms; and if they have much work to do, and very little time to say long prayers, they think about God, and offer up to him what they are doing, and ask him to bless their work.

When we are at church, or saying our morning or night prayers at home, we must be very careful to behave in a reverent manner. We must keep still, and not look about; and we must pay attention to what we are saying.

If you wanted any one to do you a favour, you would not ask it in a way that would make him think you did not care whether he granted it or not; that would be silly. And suppose some poor boy begged a penny of you, and instead of asking it in a serious manner, he laughed at you while he was begging, would you not think he did not really want food, and that he was only mocking you? And when we pretend to be saying our prayers and pay no attention to them, it is like mocking God, and we cannot expect him to accept such prayers; on the contrary, they offend him. We must remember when we kneel down that we are poor weak creatures inclined to evil, and that we are going to speak to the great God who made heaven and earth; but, at the same time, that God is our Father, and that he loves us, and will give us whatever is necessary for both body and soul, if we ask it with confidence.

SECOND MEDITATION.

On Filial Piety.

The love of God is the first of all duties, and next to it comes filial piety, which means the love of children for their parents. God has made this virtue one of his Commandments, and he has promised a long life to children who honour their parents. God calls himself our Father; and he has given to every one both a father and a mother on earth to take care of them in childhood, and bring them up in youth.

A good father and a good mother are the greatest of earthly blessings. To their children they stand in the place of God; for it is by the express command of God that parents have entire authority over their children.

A child who does not respect and obey its father and mother ceases to be a child of God, for God turns away in anger from an undutiful child.

During our childhood and youth, we owe to our parents perfect obedience. When we are grown up, we ought still to show them great respect and gratitude for all the care they took of us in our youth. We ought to return their goodness by doing all we can for them in their old age. Those who fulfil this duty are blessed by God and esteemed by men; while those who neglect it are punished by God and despised by men.

Prayer.

My God, preserve me from the sin and shame of being an undutiful child, or ever failing in respect to those whom my parents have appointed to teach me and take care of me. Give me grace never to make my parents unhappy by being wilful and disobedient. Let me never forget what I owe to their love and care; and let me never listen to any one who tells me to deceive them, or to do any thing forbidden by them. Make me, O Lord, so good that I may deserve both the blessing of my parents on earth and of my Father who is in heaven. Amen.

THIRD MEDITATION.

On Meekness and Docility.

God has said in the Gospel, "Blessed are the meek, for they shall possess the land;" which means, that those who are humble, charitable, and gentle shall without fail enter into the heavenly country.

Every body who wishes to be pleasing to God must be meek; but children far more than grown-up people have need of this virtue, because they are weak and ignorant, because they know very little, and want the help of others at all times. Grown-up people often have to rule and command others; and sometimes they are obliged to restrain or punish bad people, and then they must seem angry or severe. But little children never have to correct others: all they have to do is to obey their parents and those who are set over them; and to be kind and sweet-tempered with every one.

A disobedient, ill-humoured child is not only wicked, but also very silly; and for this reason. Bad-tempered children not only offend God, and give sorrow to their parents, but they also trouble and vex their friends, and those who take care of them, or wait on them.

Disobedient, cross children are always unhappy, because those who teach them are obliged to be often scolding or punishing them; while on the contrary, meek, obedient children are loved by every body, and seldom hear any thing but kind words from those who have the charge of them.

You must not forget that if you do not cure yourself of bad temper while you are young, by trying with all your might to be obedient and kind, and by praying to God to make you so, you will find it much harder to cure yourself when you are older. It is far easier for a child to be meek than for a grown-up person to be so. Grown-up people have more things to vex them than children have. I cannot tell you how or why this is. Little children cannot understand such things: when you are older, you will find it is so. But you can understand that it is easier work for children to cure themselves of their faults while they are young than to wait till they are grown up to begin, because the little faults will grow too, and then, instead of having to fight against little faults, we have to fight against great strong sins. Suppose, now, nobody went into the garden for a long time, for years perhaps; don't you think the weeds would grow faster than the flowers? The walks would get all covered with moss, the vegetables would die away, or be eaten up by caterpillars, snails, and slugs; the nails that held the boughs of the fruit-trees so trimly against the wall would rust and fall out; birds and wild animals would scratch up the ground, and devour the fruits and seeds, and what they spared, frosts would kill; and when the summer sun shone upon the neglected garden, all would be in disorder, and the few flowers and fruits that were left would be hidden by the weeds. Do not, therefore, think you are too young to try and conquer your faults, especially the sins of anger and impatience. Be meek, and you will be heir to a place in Paradise.

Prayer.

O Lord, give me the meekness which a child ought to have. Give me a gentle and teachable spirit, for I know that without meekness a child is not pleasing in thy sight. I can neither correct my faults nor learn what is necessary without the graces of humility and obedience, and I beg of thee, sweet Jesus, to make me meek and lowly of heart. Amen.

FOURTH MEDITATION.

On Brotherly Love.

God commands us to love all men because they are all his children; but we ought to love our own family in a more particular manner.

After our parents, our brothers and sisters should have the first place; they are our nearest relations, and they are the natural companions and friends of our childhood. God, who loves order and peace, gives his blessing to families who live peaceably and lovingly together. It is not enough to *say* you love your brothers and sisters, and to be fond of kissing them when they do just what you like; that is loving yourself, not them. If you wish to prove that you love them really and truly, you must try hard never to be cross to them; never to speak to them in a rude way; never to tell tales of them; and never to laugh at them when you see it vexes them very much. You must also be always willing to give them a share of every thing that is given to you; and never be jealous if any of them should sometimes get more presents or more praise than you do. If any of them should seem to you to be more petted than you are, say to yourself, " My Father who is in heaven knows what is best for me. Perhaps if I were too much petted, I should be spoiled."

Some little children are always ill if they eat pastry or sweets; others can eat plenty, and not be the worse for it. One child is not exactly like another. Some children can run about in the rain or the snow, and grow all the stronger for it. Others are delicate, and would catch cold (perhaps even die) if they were forced to stay out a long time in bad weather. It is the same with their souls. What does good to one may do harm to another. And you know if you have a headache, or feel a little sick, you cannot eat the things that you are accustomed to eat when you are quite well, without hurting yourself very much, and perhaps making yourself so ill that you are forced to see the doctor.

And so it is with your soul. Sometimes it would be bad for you to be petted and praised, and God knows that, and makes people take no notice of you, for fear you should grow proud, or vain, or bad tempered, or lazy, or careless about doing what is right. And so never be jealous of any one. It is not only wicked to be jealous, but is also very foolish, for it is not the way to make people like you. And children who take pleasure in seeing their brothers and sisters happy will always be happy themselves. Is it not much nicer to see people smiling than looking sour and discontented? Poor beggars who have not where to lay their heads, and poor people who work hard all day long, even when they are not strong and well, and can hardly get money enough to give food and clothes to their children with all their striving, may be forgiven if they sometimes look cross and sour. Very often they are not really discontented, only very tired and hungry, or vexed and grieved to see their children without proper clothes. God knows all they suffer, and if they bear their trials patiently, he will give them a great reward in heaven. But children who have a comfortable house to live in, good clothes, nice food, and kind people to take care of them, ought never to look cross or sour; never, never, for one minute. And if any of their brothers or sisters, or their cousins or young companions, receive presents or praise while they get nothing, they ought to be quite glad to see their little friends so happy, and they ought to rejoice with them; and in that way they will enjoy the present as much as if it were their own. But I dare say you are never jealous, and are always willing that your brothers and sisters and little playfellows should have the best of every thing. I know many generous, good children, who are never selfish, and are always willing for others to be preferred before them. I hope you are like them, and that you do not know what it is to feel jealous. Jealousy is an ugly, nasty, mean thing. Never let it get into your dear little heart; and pray to the

Sacred Heart of our Lord, and the most pure Heart of Mary, to keep this vice far from you, now, and all your life long.

Prayer.

My God, make me always love those whom it is my duty to love. Give me grace to behave so kindly to my brothers and sisters that they may never have cause to doubt of my love. Drive far from this house and family all quarrelling and disputing; and let thy holy angels dwell herein to keep us in peace; and may thy blessing be upon us now and for ever; through our Lord Jesus Christ. Amen.

FIFTH MEDITATION.

On the Love of our Neighbour.

All men are equal in the sight of God. St. Paul says many times that there is no respect of persons with God; which means, that God values us according to the state of our souls, and that he cares nothing about our place in the world, of what country we are, whether high or low by birth, whether rich or poor.

We ought, therefore, neither to be

proud if God has caused us to be born noble or rich, nor should we be envious and jealous if we are born in a lower station, or in poverty. For the sake of peace and order, there must be certain persons chosen to govern countries and provinces, whom we call emperors, kings, queens, dukes, governors, presidents, &c. Besides this, there are certain families whose ancestors did some service to their king or country long ago, and who were rewarded for it by having a title or name of honour given to them, which their children and their children's children were to be called by for many generations. Then there are families who have been so fortunate as to keep the lands left in their charge hundreds of years ago by their forefathers; while there are others who have lost their lands in a good cause. I cannot explain all this to you properly now, but you will understand it when you are old enough to read history. And besides these, there are many people whose forefathers lost their property through waste and carelessness. Some children are inclined to destroy books and furniture; to spoil their clothes, to lose their things, and never take the trouble of looking for them; to be very dainty about what they eat; to spend all their money on themselves; to be lazy, careless, and wasteful. Now, if rich children grow up with all these bad habits, when they are men and women, one of these two things will happen: either they will never have any thing to give away to those who want help, and so they will not gain the blessing of God; or they will waste and lose what belongs to them, and make themselves and their children poor.

But sometimes rich people get poor without any fault of their own; and many people are born poor. Our Lord chose to be born poor, as you know. His blessed Mother was very poor, and worked with her hands for her living. And when rich people are very good, they often think of this, and it prevents them from being proud, and makes them not only be kind to the poor, but really respect them.

There is another thing to be remembered. We are not all born alike, in ourselves. Some children are strong, others are weak; some are clever, and others dull; some are brave, and others timid; some active, and others lazy. Now remember all children can cure themselves of their faults; and if we cannot change ourselves altogether, we can improve ourselves. If we are born short, we cannot make ourselves tall; if we are born dull, we cannot make ourselves bright; but I will tell you what we can do. We can be industrious and painstaking and thoughtful and kind; nay, we can be brave too, if we choose to try hard, and that is better than being clever and idle, or bold and selfish. We can all speak the truth, and avoid saying unkind things, and do all the good we can to every body; and if we act so, our friends will love us, and all who know us well will trust us, and the poor will bless us, and what is best of all, our Lord will look down from heaven upon us with love, and say to us, " Blessed are the poor in spirit, for theirs is the kingdom of heaven."

Prayer.

O God of mercy who hast commanded us to love and help one another, make me tender-hearted to all in sorrow or poverty, and kind to every body. Grant me grace when I am older to do good to my neighbour, so that when I die, I may find a place prepared for me in heaven. Amen.

SIXTH MEDITATION.

On Truth.

God being Truth itself, nothing is more hateful in his sight than lying. The first falsehood that ever was spoken was invented by Satan. He told a lie to Eve in Paradise in order to make her disobey God.

Our Lord says in the Gospel that the devil is the father of lying. We ought, therefore, to have a great horror of every thing false and untrue. To love the truth is to love God, who is the Source and Author of truth; and if we love truth, it follows that we shall hate what is contrary to it. Remember, then, that we must always speak the truth, and that it is forbidden to tell a falsehood for any thing in the world. Never be tempted to tell even a very little untruth to excuse yourself, if you are afraid of being punished. One story leads to another, for it is a hard thing to own that you have told a falsehood. Lying is always considered a mean, low vice, and every one is ashamed when they are found out telling stories.

Some children suffer a great deal because they have told a little story for want of thought, and then have not had the courage to own it, but have been tempted to add a second sin to the first by persevering in a false tale. If you have broken or lost any thing, you should always tell of it as soon as you can. You may forget it, and some innocent person might get blamed for what is really your fault. It is far better to bear the punishment that you deserve for being careless or awkward than to hide the mischief you have done, and then be tormented by the fear that it will be found out some day, or that some body else will be blamed without deserving it. To let another be blamed for what is really our own fault is mean and cowardly; and if we do it knowingly, it is just as bad as telling a story. One can tell a falsehood without saying a word. But now I must tell you that there are times when one need not say all one knows.

Sometimes telling a thing would do mischief, or get somebody into trouble. In that case you are allowed to keep silence; unless, indeed, you should be questioned by your parents or teachers. If so, and you wish not to tell tales, you must beg them not to ask you any questions; but if they insist on knowing every thing, why then there is no help for it; you will be obliged to speak out, and tell the whole truth plainly.

Some children are always chattering, and get the habit of saying every thing that comes into their heads. This fault looks like openness, but it often leads to want of truthfulness; and for this reason: people who are always talking have not time to think of what they are saying till the words come out of their mouth; and so they say things that they don't quite mean. They make a great fuss about every thing, and make things seem different to what they really are. Such children, if they knock themselves, or fall down and hurt themselves a little, will cry out as much as if they were very badly hurt; or if they are not quite pleased with a person, will call them " very cross," or " very unkind," though they know all the time that person is not " cross" or " unkind." If they speak of any thing they have seen, they will make it out to be larger or smaller, or much better or much worse, than it really is; and if you ask them a question that only requires yes or no, they will go on chattering about a great many things that have nothing to do with the matter, which is tiresome, and sometimes very provoking, and instead of helping to make people come at the truth of a thing, often perplexes and deceives them.

Chattering people do harm in another way. If their mamma, or some one who takes care of them, desires them not to speak about a thing, they will forget, and begin chattering about it, and perhaps vex some one by their foolish talking, or do some mischief by telling what they ought not to tell. Some children are very fond of secrets: others do not like them. I have remarked that it is generally those who like them best that never can keep them long. Now remember that if any one offers to tell you a secret, and asks you to promise not to tell, you should always answer that you tell every thing to to your parents, and that you cannot promise not to tell *them*, but that you will promise not to tell any one else.

Secrets are tiresome things, and I advise you never to have any if you can help it; but mind, it is a shameful thing to betray a secret, and if we promise not to tell a thing, we never should break our word. No one who does so is ever trusted, whether they are children or grown-up people. There are some children who, when they are angry with one of their young friends, will repeat the things that had been told to them before they were angry. That is very bad, indeed, and children who cannot keep their tongues quiet when they are in a passion will be always in danger of losing the friendship of their young companions; and if they do not cure themselves of this evil habit while they are young, they will never have any real friends when they are grown up, because people will be afraid to trust them.

Make a resolution, therefore, to speak the truth at all times; and if you should ever find yourself saying any thing that you feel is not quite true, check yourself at once, and keep silence.

Prayer.

O Eternal Wisdom and Fountain of Truth, make me feel how beautiful thou art, and grant me all my life through to love what is true, and to despise what is false; through our Lord Jesus Christ. Amen.

SEVENTH MEDITATION.

On Pride.

Pride is a vice so strong that it made

Lucifer and his companions rebel against God and lose their place in heaven. So dreadful a passion is pride, that when it gets a firm hold of the heart, it can change it in one instant, just as it changed the beautiful angels into frightful devils. When we see a child who is generally humble giving way to a sudden temptation to be proud, we see such a change come over that poor little creature, that we feel inclined to say to ourselves, " Can that be the same child who a short time ago was as gentle as a dove ?" There is as much difference between a person whose heart is full of humility, and the same person when his heart is full of pride, as there is between a wolf and a lamb. Humility is the most necessary of all virtues : without it, whatever good qualities we may have will count for nothing in the sight of God. Our Lord Jesus Christ came down from heaven, not only to die for us, but also to set before us the pattern of what a perfect Christian should be. The saints have tried to walk in his footsteps ; which means, that they have tried to copy their Divine Master as much as they possibly could. Some saints have imitated him in certain things, and not in others; but all have copied him in being humble. The humility of our Lord Jesus is far more wonderful than all the miracles he worked while he was on earth. He was the Creator and sovereign Lord of all things, yet he took upon himself the form of a servant. He might have come into the world as the son of a king, but he chose to be thought the son of a carpenter. It would have been a great act of humility in him if he had chosen to be born the son of some rich man; but he would do more—he would be so poor that he had not where to lay his head. And he ended a life of humiliations by letting his own creatures put him to a cruel death, though he could, if he pleased, with one word have destroyed all those wicked men who nailed him to the cross. O wonderful humility of Jesus! Well might he be called the Lamb of God! With such an example before our eyes, how can we be proud? We are nothing but creatures, and shall we desire to be treated with more honour than our Creator?

Vanity is not so great a sin as pride, but it is, perhaps, even more difficult to cure. Pride makes people think so highly of themselves that they do not care much what others think or say of them. Vanity makes people more anxious to have other people's good opinion than their own. Proud people sometimes seem humble enough till they are set on fire by something that they consider an insult or a slight, but vain people cannot help showing their vanity at all times. Vanity makes people restless unless they are taken notice of and put forward : they cannot be happy unless they are made a fuss about. It is not enough for them to know that their friends love them and value them: they cannot be contented unless strangers, and people they don't really care for, should see all their good qualities. Vain people would not care to be pretty, or clever, or rich, or well dressed, unless they could show off their fine things before others. This is silly and contemptible, for it matters very little what people think of us: it makes us neither better nor worse than we really are. And you may be sure that those grown-up people who take notice of children because they look pretty or wear handsome clothes always forget them as soon as they are out of sight. And is such notice as that worth having? There is nothing more silly than to care for fine clothes; they are not even part of oneself. The beautiful feathers of a bird do really belong to it, but dress is not our own. And the prettiest dress that ever was made is not half so pretty as a butterfly or a common wild flower that grows in the hedges. People who have sense take more pleasure in looking at a daisy or a buttercup than at a child decked out in finery. Make a resolution, then, never to be proud or vain, and recollect that all we have comes from God, and that if we happen to be highborn, rich, clever, or pretty, these things are gifts from our Creator which he means us to use, not to please ourselves, but to do good with, and that we shall have to give an account of what use we have put them to, when God calls us before his throne to be judged.

Prayer.

O Lamb of God, who takest away the sins of the world, destroy in me all pride and vanity, and give me grace to know my own weakness and nothingness. Sweet Jesus, meek and humble of heart, make my heart like unto thy Sacred Heart. Amen.

EIGHTH MEDITATION.

On Temperance.

Gluttony is a shameful vice, unworthy not only of a Christian, but of a rational creature. Religion commands us to be temperate, and consequently temperance must be one of the virtues necessary for salvation. Reason tells us that temperance is necessary for our bodily health; for we find that people who give way to intemperance make themselves ill, suffer dreadful pain, and never live to be old.

We are obliged to be sober on pain of destroying the health both of our souls and bodies. But something more than sobriety is required of us in order to be pleasing in the sight of God. Those who eat or drink to excess are called gluttons or drunkards, and such persons are reckoned to be great sinners by every one. But without eating or drinking to excess, we can be guilty of the sin of gluttony to a certain degree very easily in two different ways. I mean, either by giving way to a habit of being dainty and hard to please as regards what we eat, or by eating more than we really want, when we get any thing we think particularly nice.

Some children are very much tempted to greediness, others think very little about what they eat. The reason of this is, that some children are taught in the nursery neither to be dainty nor greedy; while others are encouraged in all their fancies, and never checked in self-indulgence, unless they make themselves ill.

When children are weak and delicate, sometimes a doctor orders them to have nice things to make them eat enough to strengthen them; that is quite another thing. St. Timothy was a Bishop who always drank water; but when he got ill, St. Paul wrote to tell him to take a little wine to make him strong. But doctors seldom order people to eat good things when they have no appetite; on the contrary, if we are not hungry, that is generally a sign that we are better without food. When sick children require strengthening, they have to take bitter stuff called tonics, or cod-liver oil; some take raw eggs or asses' milk; neither of which are particularly nice. And as to their food, if the doctor orders them to have poultry, jellies, and *blanc-mange* very often, because those things are nice and nourishing, they generally get tired of them, and care very little about eating them. And so I do not think sick children are in much danger of being greedy. Poor little creatures! they would gladly exchange all their nice things for the good appetite which makes a healthy child enjoy a bit of dry bread. And, in general, I am afraid it is the strong, healthy children who give way to greediness. This is both wrong and foolish in them; their Creator has given them a body so strong and healthy, that they can take exercise out of doors, no matter what the weather is, and so come to their meals hungry enough to eat comfortably any wholesome food that happens to be set before them. This is, in itself, a great blessing, and one which no grown-up people enjoy unless they have practised temperance and self-denial all their lives. It is therefore ungrateful to complain if the food prepared for them does not happen to be exactly what they would have chosen. So long as it is clean, good of its kind, and cooked in a wholesome manner, we have no right to wish for more, or to be discontented because it does not please our taste as well as certain other dishes. And you may be sure that plain food, when one is hungry, is far more enjoyable than the greatest dainties are, when one has no inclination to eat. For this reason, it is foolish to pamper the appetite when we are young, and so risk injuring our health, and obliging ourselves to be very particular about what we eat when we are grown up. Make a resolution, therefore, to curb yourself whenever you feel tempted to the sin of greediness, even in trifles; and on all the days of abstinence appointed by the Church, take cheerfully the food that is provided for you.

Prayer.

O most sweet Jesus, who for us didst fast forty days, give me grace always to receive thankfully the food that is set before me, and make me use all thy gifts with moderation. Amen.

NINTH MEDITATION.
On Diligence.

God has commanded us to practise self-denial not only in eating and drinking, but also in every thing that concerns our own comfort and ease. One of the reasons why it is difficult for rich people to go to heaven is, that money gives them the power of leading idle, slothful, self-indulgent lives. Of course a poor person may lead an idle, slothful life too; but their lives will not be easy and comfortable, if they are idle. For if they do not work hard, they cannot earn money enough to get good food and good clothes, and a decent place to live in. When poor people are idle, they soon come to rags and starvation; but rich people can be slothful. and study their own ease and pleasure from morning to night, without suffering for it much in this world. It is true such people are called selfish, and nobody respects or admires them, and few people like them. They don't care for that, because they are wrapped up in themselves. But if they should be ill, they will suffer more than others, from never having learnt to bear pain or inconvenience patiently; and when they come to die, they will be tormented by looking back upon all the years they have spent in sloth, and they will wish they had done more good to their neighbour, and thought less of their own comfort. Diligence is the virtue opposed to sloth. It is a virtue children generally find hard, because it is natural to us to like to be idle and fond of amusement. Children who are well brought up learn how to work properly when they are young, so that by the time they are grown up, they gain the habit of doing something useful every day, and get to like work, and to feel uncomfortable if they are required to spend much time in idleness. The kind of work expected from rich children is study. All little girls, whether rich or poor, ought to learn needlework; but most of them find it so easy, that they look upon it rather as an amusement than a study. All poor children ought to have time to learn to read, to cast up easy sums, and to do common household work properly. But sometimes poor people are obliged to let their children go out to work for their living while they are very young, and in that case the poor little things have no chance of learning what every body living in a Christian country, in these days, ought to know. This is a sad thing; and it is the duty of rich people to encourage poor schools, and to help industrious poor people, who would be glad to send their children to school, if they could manage to get enough to live upon themselves.

Those children whose parents are rich enough and generous enough to pay a great deal of money for their education, ought to be very thankful for this advantage, and remember that it is a gift from

God for which they will have to give an account when they die. Suppose a rich lady gave her children a quantity of beautiful presents which cost a great deal of money, and the children set no value on them, but threw them aside and lost them, would you not say those children were ungrateful and foolish? Now young people who refuse to learn when their parents have provided them with books and teachers, act just as ungratefully, and even more foolishly, than children who throw away costly toys.

If you do not try to learn while you are young, it will be harder work to study when you are grown up. Besides, you are not sure you will always have the same opportunities of learning. There are many things which are not hard to learn, if one begins them in the right way when we are young, but which are very troublesome indeed to learn after one is grown up; and then you may be forced to lay aside your books just as you are beginning to wish to be clever. You might be ill for some time, or you may have things to do which will interfere with study at the very moment when you are intending to make up for lost time. Besides this, children who neglect their studies grow up either inactive or over-fond of amusement; and idle people, though they may be good-natured enough to wish to be of use to their fellow creatures, cannot make time to fulfil their good intentions. People who have a habit of wasting time can do no works of charity among the poor without neglecting their friends or their duties at home. Make a resolution to get up in the morning directly you are called; not to loiter or dawdle while you are dressing or going to bed; and to be diligent at all your studies, and in any work you are required to do.

Prayer.

Sweet Jesus, who didst not disdain to spend thy youth working with thy hands in a carpenter's shop and in a poor cottage, grant me grace to be diligent in all my employments, and to spend my life in doing such things as thy providence shall call me to perform. Amen.

LAST MEDITATION.
On Temptation.

The devil, who is always trying to injure us, often fills our hearts with temptations. A temptation is a wish to do wrong. God allows us to be tempted in order to try us, and to give us an opportunity of gaining the reward which he prepares for all who fight against temptation. The best people are sometimes tempted to do wrong, but they do not give way to their inclinations. On the contrary, they resist the temptation; and by so doing, become stronger and holier than they were before. Thus all the attempts of the devil to do them harm come to nothing, or rather increase their merits.

But we must remember that we are so weak and naturally inclined to evil, that we can do nothing without the help of Almighty God. Therefore it would be of no use for us to try and fight against temptations without praying for strength to do it. If we forget that we are poor weak creatures, and fancy we can do what is right by our strength, we shall be sure to fall. Sometimes God allows us to fall in order to cure us of pride and presumption. If we get to think ourselves very good, and to fancy that it is quite impossible for us to do any thing very bad, God will allow Satan to tempt us in some way we do not expect; and then, if we forget to pray for help, we shall give way to the temptation, and do something very wrong. Now, if this misfortune should happen to you, do not be frightened or cast down, nor fancy that God has deserted you, and that Satan is too strong for you. No, no; God never deserts any one who calls upon him; and as for the devil, he cannot hurt us the least bit, unless we let him have his own way, and like his company so well that we neglect to ask God to drive him far from us. And so, if you should have the misfortune to give way to temptation and do something very bad, it may end in your getting good out of evil, if you will but be humble and patient, and turn yourself to God directly, saying something like this: "O my God, I forgot what a weak, bad creature I am. I was foolish enough to fancy myself good, and now, see what I have done. Forgive me this great sin, O Lord, and make me humble and watchful for the future." There is another thing you must be prepared for. When any one makes a resolution to be very good, that displeases Satan, and he resolves to do all he can to hinder him from keeping his good resolution. He behaves to us just as he did to Adam and Eve. He will tempt us to be angry, or sulky, or proud, or greedy, or lazy, or untruthful, perhaps many times every day; or he may let us alone for some time, and when

we are getting to think it easy to be good,
he will tempt us just when we least expect
it; and then, as I said before, if we
forget to ask for God's grace to help us,
we shall listen to the tempter, and go
wrong. Then we shall feel unhappy; but
we must take courage, and beg God to
forgive us, and recommend ourselves to
our Blessed Lady and our angel guardian,
and then make a fresh resolution to
be good, and begin over again. In time
we shall get strong. Practice makes perfect,
says the proverb. You must not be
surprised if you should fall many times,
because, besides the temptations which
come from the devil, there are also the
temptations which come from our own
nature, and they are often more difficult
to conquer than any others, because they
seem to belong to us, to be a part of ourselves,
and very often we are blind to
them, or so used to them that we cannot
see how bad they are. Some children have
a proud sulky nature; others are inclined
to be passionate and hasty; others are
sweet-tempered, but idle or lazy; others
are dainty in eating, or selfish in their
ways; in short, some have one fault, and
some have another, in their own natures;
and the temptations that come from our

own hearts will be the ones that will require the most perseverance to get them under. God has promised a great reward to those who triumph over temptation. The martyrs were tried by cruel torments; and if they had not held out courageously, they would not have received their crowns. Try, then, dear child, to fight against temptation: if it should seem hard work, think of the joy you will have when holy angels carry you away from this world, and the gates of heaven open before you, and you enter into that lovely land where you will see Blessed Mary and the saints and angels rejoicing and singing, all ready to welcome you and conduct you to the throne of Almighty God, who will say to those who have laboured hard to do his will: "Well done, good and faithful servant; enter thou into the joy of thy Lord."

Prayer.

O sweet Lord Jesus Christ, let the memory of thy passion make me cheerfully suffer all temptations and pains here for thy dear love, and let my soul always long after the happiness and glory which thou hast prepared in heaven for those who love and serve thee. Amen.

VESPERS.

VESPERS are the evening prayers of the Church, but they are generally said in the afternoon. Vespers form part of what is called the Great Office, which is a collection of psalms, hymns, prayers, and portions of Holy Scripture, arranged in order. Priests, and some monks and nuns, are the only people who are obliged to say the Office. In the Psalms, holy David says, "Seven times a day do I praise thee;" and the Office of the Church is arranged so as to imitate the holy king's example. There are seven portions of the Office, divided so that they may be repeated at different hours: they are called Matins and Lauds, Prime, Terce, Sext, None, Vespers, and Compline.

When you are older, you will find books that will explain the meaning of these names; and if you should learn Latin by and by, you will be able to read the Office yourself. It has beautiful hymns in it, and the lessons and prayers are very beautiful too. The psalms you will read in English, I hope, before you are grown up.

Vespers and Compline are often sung together on Sunday at church, either as afternoon or evening prayers; and that is the reason that I have put them into your prayer-book.

They are always sung or recited in Latin in public worship; but when we repeat them at home, we may say them either in English or Latin, as we please. When the Office is said in a church or chapel, the choir (or the congregation) divide into two companies; and one set of people sing or recite one verse of the psalm, and the others answer with the next verse. In the days when St. Ambrose was Bishop of Milan, more than a thousand years ago, the people used to sing psalms and hymns in the great church at Milan so beautifully, that St. Augustine said the grand and sweet sounds lifted his heart up to heaven.

Prayer before Vespers.

O dear Lord Jesus, who wast buried in the evening, and didst in the evening eat the Last Supper with thy disciples, instituting the most Blessed Sacrament of the altar, give us grace to assist at this holy office of Vespers, said at the close of the day in remembrance of those great and solemn events. We desire to recite the five psalms of the Vespers in honour of the five Wounds made in thy most sacred Body; and we beg of thee to pardon all the sins we have committed by means of our five senses this day; and we beg thee to give us grace to amend our faults during the new week we have just begun. Amen.

Vespers for Sundays.

"Our Father" and "Hail Mary" being said in silence, the priest sings aloud,

℣. Deus, in adjutorium meum intende.
℟. Domine, ad adjuvandum me festina.

Which means,

O God, make speed to save me.
O Lord, make haste to help me.
Glory be to the Father, &c.

Before each of the Psalms an Antiphon is said. When you are old enough to have a Vesper Book, you will learn to find out the places, and read the proper Antiphons for each day. I have put into this little book the Antiphons and Hymn which are appointed to be said on the Holy Innocents' Day. They will serve for you to read while the proper Antiphons and Hymn are being sung.

First Antiphon.

Herod, enraged, slew many children in Bethlehem of Juda, the city of David.

Psalm cix. *Dixit Dominus.*

1 The Lord said to my Lord: Sit thou at my right hand:

2 Until I make thine enemies: thy footstool.

3 The Lord shall send forth the rod

of thy power from out of Sion: rule thou in the midst of thine enemies.

4 Thine shall be the dominion in the day of thy power, amid the brightness of the Saints: from the womb, before the day-star, have I begotten thee.

5 The Lord hath sworn, and will not repent: Thou art a priest for ever according to the order of Melchisedec.

6 The Lord upon thy right hand: hath overthrown kings in the day of his wrath.

7 He shall judge among the nations, he shall fulfil destructions: he shall smite in sunder the heads in the land of many.

8 He shall drink of the brook in the way: therefore shall he lift up his head.

Glory be to the Father, &c.

Second Antiphon.

Herod killed many children, from two years old and under, on account of the Lord.

Psalm cx. *Confitebor tibi.*

1 I will praise thee, O Lord, with my whole heart: in the assembly of the just, and in the congregation.

2 Great are the works of the Lord: sought out are they unto all his pleasure.

3 His work is his praise, and his honour: and his justice endureth for ever and ever.

4 The merciful and gracious Lord hath left a memorial of his marvellous works: he hath given meat to them that fear him.

5 He shall ever be mindful of his covenant: he shall show forth unto his people the power of his works:

6 That he may give them the heritage of the gentiles: the works of his hands are judgment and truth.

7 Faithful are all his commandments; they stand fast for ever and ever: they are done in truth and equity.

8 He hath sent redemption unto his people: he hath commanded his covenant for ever.

9 Holy and terrible is his name: the fear of the Lord is the beginning of wisdom.

10 A good understanding have all they that do thereafter: his praise endureth for ever and ever.

Glory be to the Father, &c.

Third Antiphon.

Their angels always see the face of the Father.

Psalm cxi. *Beatus vir.*

1 Blessed is the man, that feareth the Lord: in his commandments he shall have great delight.

2 His seed shall be mighty upon earth: the generation of the righteous shall be blessed.

3 Glory and riches shall be in his house: and his justice endureth for ever and ever.

4 Unto the righteous there hath risen up light in the darkness: he is merciful, compassionate, and just.

5 Acceptable is the man who is merciful and lendeth, he shall order his words with judgment: for he shall not be moved for ever.

6 The just man shall be in everlasting remembrance: he shall not be afraid for evil report.

7 His heart is prepared to hope in the Lord; his heart is fixed: he shall not be moved until he look down upon his enemies.

8 He hath dispersed abroad, he hath given to the poor; his justice endureth for ever and ever: his horn shall be exalted in glory.

9 The sinner shall see it and be wroth;

he shall gnash with his teeth, and consume away: the desire of the wicked shall perish.

Glory be to the Father, &c.

Fourth Antiphon.

A voice was heard in Rama, lamentation and great mourning; Rachel bewailing her children.

Psalm cxii. *Laudate pueri.*

1 Praise the Lord, ye children: praise ye the name of the Lord.

2 Blessed be the name of the Lord: from this time forth for evermore.

3 From the rising up of the sun unto the going down of the same: the name of the Lord is worthy to be praised.

4 The Lord is high above all nations: and his glory above the heavens.

5 Who is like unto the Lord our God, who dwelleth on high: and regardeth the things that are lowly in heaven and in earth?

6 Who raiseth up the needy from the earth: and lifteth the poor from off the dunghill:

7 That he may set him with the princes: even with the princes of his people.

8 Who maketh the barren woman to dwell in her house: the joyful mother of children.

Glory be to the Father, &c.

Fifth Antiphon.

Under the throne of God all the saints cry out, Revenge our blood, O our God.

Psalm cxiii. *In exitu Israel.*

1 When Israel came out of Egypt: the house of Jacob from among a strange people.

2 Judah was made his sanctuary: and Israel his dominion.

3 The sea beheld, and fled: Jordan was turned back.

4 The mountains skipped like rams: and the little hills like the lambs of the flock.

5 What aileth thee, O thou sea, that thou fleddest: and thou Jordan, that thou wast turned back?

6 Ye mountains, that ye skipped like rams: and ye little hills like the lambs of the flock?

7 At the presence of the Lord the earth

was moved: at the presence of the God of Jacob.

8 Who turned the rock into a standing water: and the stony hill into a flowing stream.

9 Not unto us, O Lord, not unto us: but unto thy name give the glory.

10 For thy mercy and for thy truth's sake: lest the Gentiles should say, Where is their God?

11 But our God is in heaven: he hath done whatsoever he would.

12 The idols of the Gentiles are silver and gold: the work of the hands of men.

13 They have mouths, and they shall not speak: they have eyes, and they shall not see.

14 They have ears, and they shall not hear: they have noses, and they shall not smell.

15 They have hands, and they shall not feel; they have feet, and they shall not walk: neither shall they speak through their throat.

16 Let those that make them become like unto them: and all such as put their trust in them.

17 The house of Israel hath hoped in the Lord: he is their helper and protector.

18 The house of Aaron hath hoped in the Lord: he is their helper and protector.

19 They that fear the Lord, have hoped in the Lord: he is their helper and protector.

20 The Lord hath been mindful of us: and hath blessed us.

21 He hath blessed the house of Israel: he hath blessed the house of Aaron.

22 He hath blessed all that fear the Lord: the least together with the greatest.

23 May the Lord add blessings upon you: upon you, and upon your children.

24 Blessed be ye of the Lord: who hath made heaven and earth.

25 The heaven of heavens is the Lord's; but the earth hath he given to the children of men.

26 The dead shall not praise thee, O Lord: neither all they that go down into hell.

27 But we who live, bless the Lord: from this time forth for evermore.

Glory be to the Father, &c.

This last Psalm is not said very often; instead of it Psalm cxvi., "Laudate Dominum," is frequently said. Sometimes other Psalms are said in the place of some of those appointed for Sundays.

Psalm cxvi. *Laudate Dominum.*

1 Praise the Lord, all ye Gentiles: praise him, all ye people:

2 For his mercy is confirmed upon us: and the truth of the Lord endureth for ever.

At the Little Chapter.

Innocents were slain for Christ; sucking babes were murdered by a wicked king. They follow the Lamb without spot, always saying, Glory be to thee, O Lord.

Thanks be to God.

Hymn.

Lovely flowers of martyrs, hail!
   Smitten by the tyrant foe
On life's threshold,—as the gale
   Strews the roses ere they blow.

First to die for Christ, sweet lambs!
   At the very altar ye,
With your fatal crowns and palms,
   Sport in your simplicity.

Honour, glory, virtue, merit,
   Be to thee, O Virgin's Son!
With the Father, and the Spirit,
   While eternal ages run.

Another Hymn.

When it reach'd the tyrant's ear,
  Brooding anxious all alone,
That the King of kings was near,
  Who should sit on David's throne;

Stung with madness, straight he cries,
  " Treason threatens—draw the
    sword!
Rebels all around us rise!
  Drown the cradles deep in blood."

What is cruel Herod's gain,
  Though a thousand babes he slay?—
Christ, amid a thousand slain,
  Is in safety borne away.

Honour, glory, virtue, merit,
  Be to thee, O Virgin's Son!
With the Father, and the Spirit,
  While eternal ages run.

After the Hymn two short sentences are said, called the "Versicle" and "Response;" then the Antiphon for the "Magnificat." You can say:

V. Let my prayer ascend, O Lord.
R. Like incense in thy sight.
Hail Mary.

VESPERS.

Magnificat, or Song of the B. V. Mary.

1 My soul doth magnify : the Lord.

2 And my spirit hath rejoiced : in God my Saviour.

3 For he hath regarded the lowliness of his handmaid : for behold from henceforth all generations shall call me blessed.

4 For he that is mighty hath done great things unto me : and holy is his name.

5 And his mercy is from generation to generation : unto them that fear him.

6 He hath showed strength with his arm : he hath scattered the proud in the imagination of their heart.

7 He hath put down the mighty from their seat : and hath exalted the humble.

8 He hath filled the hungry with good things : and the rich he hath sent empty away.

9 He hath holpen his servant Israel : being mindful of his mercy.

10 As he spake unto our fathers : to Abraham and his seed for ever.

Glory be to the Father, &c.

V. The Lord be with you.

R. And with thy spirit.

Then follow some prayers, during which you can say any you like of the prayers set down below.

VESPERS.

Let us pray.

Bend thine ear, O Lord, we beseech thee, to our prayers, and enlighten the darkness of our minds by the grace of thy visitation. Amen.

Grant, we beseech thee, Almighty God, that the new birth of thy only-begotten Son in the flesh may deliver us from the old slavery under the yoke of sin. Amen.

Almighty and eternal God, direct our actions according to thy pleasure, that in the name of thy beloved Son we may be enabled to abound in good works. Amen.

O God, who seest us void of all strength, preserve us without and within, that our bodies may be secured from all adversities, and our souls purified from evil thoughts. Through our Lord Jesus Christ. Amen.

O God, from whom are all holy desires, right counsels, and just works, give to thy servants that peace which the world cannot give; that our hearts being fixed on thy commands, and the fear of enemies being removed, the times through thy protection may be peaceable. Through our Lord Jesus Christ. Amen.

VESPERS. 87

V. The Lord be with you.
R. And with thy spirit.
V. Let us bless the Lord.
R. Thanks be to God.
V. May the souls of the faithful through the mercy of God rest in peace.
R. Amen.

Our Father (*said in silence*).

V. The Lord give us his peace.
R. And eternal life.   Amen.

COMPLINE.

Compline is the last hour of the Office, and the word *compline* means 'the finishing,' or 'the end.' The first three Psalms tell of our trust in God when we are going to lie down in our beds to take our rest, and of the comfort given to those who hope in God, and of his promises to take care of his children. The last Psalm tells us to offer up our hearts to God, if we should wake in the night; and it reminds us of the practice of the first Christians, who used to rise during the night to pray.

Jube, domne, benedicere.
Pray, father, give me your blessing.

The Blessing.

May the Lord Almighty grant us a quiet night, and a perfect end.
R. Amen.

VESPERS.

Short Lesson.

Brethren, be sober, and watch: because your adversary, the devil, as a roaring lion goeth about, seeking whom he may devour; whom resist ye strong in faith. But do thou, O Lord, have mercy on us.

R. Thanks be to God.
V. Our help is in the name of the Lord.
R. Who hath made heaven and earth.

Our Father, &c. (*said in silence*).

Confiteor, &c. said by the Priest. Choir answers:

May almighty God have mercy upon thee, forgive thee thy sins, and bring thee to life everlasting.

R. Amen.

Choir repeats the Confession:

I confess to almighty God, to blessed Mary ever Virgin, to blessed Michael the Archangel, to blessed John the Baptist, to the holy Apostles Peter and Paul, to all the Saints, and to you, father: that I have sinned exceedingly in thought, word, and deed: through my fault, through my fault, through my most grievous fault. Therefore I beseech the blessed Mary ever Virgin, blessed Michael the Archangel, blessed John the Baptist, the holy Apostles Peter and Paul, all the Saints, and you, father, to pray to the Lord our God for me.

Priest gives the Absolution:

May almighty God have mercy upon you, forgive you your sins, and bring you to life everlasting.

R. Amen.

May the almighty and merciful Lord grant us pardon, absolution, and remission of our sins.

R. Amen.

Ant. Have mercy on me, O Lord, and hear my prayer.

Psalm iv. *Cum invocarem.*

1 When I called upon him, the God of my justice heard me: when I was in distress, thou didst enlarge me.

2 Have mercy upon me: and hear my prayer.

3 O ye sons of men, how long will ye be dull of heart: why do ye love vanity, and seek after lying?

4 Know ye also that the Lord hath exalted his holy one: the Lord will hear me, when I cry unto him.

5 Be ye angry, and sin not: the things which ye say in your hearts, be sorry for upon your beds.

6 Offer up the sacrifice of justice, and hope in the Lord: there are many that say, Who showeth us good things?

7 The light of thy countenance, O Lord, is signed upon us: thou hast put gladness in my heart.

8 By the fruit of their corn and wine and oil: are they multiplied.

9 In peace in the self-same: I will sleep and take my rest.

10 For thou only, O Lord: hast established me in hope.

Glory be to the Father, &c.

Psalm xxx. *In te, Domine, speravi.*

1 In thee, O Lord, have I hoped, let me never be confounded: deliver me in thy justice.

2 Incline thine ear unto me: make haste to deliver me.

3 Be thou, my God, my protector, and a house of refuge: that thou mayest save me.

4 For thou art my strength and my refuge: and for thy name's sake, thou wilt lead me and nourish me.

5 Thou wilt bring me out of this snare, that they have laid for me: for thou art my protector.

6 Into thy hands I commend my spirit:

thou hast redeemed me, O Lord, the God of truth.

Glory be to the Father, &c.

Psalm xc. *Qui habitat.*

1 He that dwelleth in the help of the Most High : shall abide under the protection of the God of heaven.

2 He shall say unto the Lord, Thou art my upholder, and my refuge: my God, in him will I hope.

3 For he hath delivered me from the snare of the hunters: and from the sharp word.

4 He shall overshadow thee with his shoulders: and under his wings shalt thou trust.

5 His truth shall compass thee with a shield: thou shalt not be afraid for the terror of the night:

6 For the arrow that flieth in the day, for the plague that walketh in the darkness: for the assault of the evil one in the noon-day.

7 A thousand shall fall at thy side, and ten thousand at thy right hand: but it shall not come nigh thee.

8 But with thine eyes shalt thou behold: and shalt see the reward of the wicked.

9 For thou, O Lord, art my hope : thou hast set thy refuge very high.

10 There shall no evil approach unto thee : nor shall the scourge come nigh thy dwelling.

11 For he hath given his angels charge over thee : to keep thee in all thy ways.

12 In their hands shall they bear thee up : lest haply thou dash thy foot against a stone.

13 Thou shalt walk upon the asp and the basilisk : the lion and the dragon shalt thou tread under thy feet.

14 Because he hath hoped in me, I will deliver him : I will protect him, because he hath known my name.

15 He shall cry unto me, and I will hear him : I am with him in trouble, I will deliver him, and glorify him.

16 With length of days will I fill him : and I will show unto him my salvation.

Glory be to the Father, &c.

Psalm cxxxiii. *Ecce nunc.*

1 Behold now, bless ye the Lord : all ye servants of the Lord.

2 Who stand in the house of the Lord : in the courts of the house of our God.

3 Lift up your hands by night to the holy places : and bless the Lord.

4 May the Lord out of Sion bless thee : who hath made heaven and earth.

Glory be to the Father, &c.

Ant. Have mercy on me, O Lord, and graciously hear my prayer.

Hymn.

Before the daylight dies away,
Maker of all, we humbly pray,
That thou, from danger and from wrong,
Wilt deign to guard us all night long.

Let all bad dreams far from us fly;
Let no vain fancies make us sigh;
Let not the foe our sleep molest;
Guarded by thee, calm be our rest.

Grant this, O Father, great and good,
And Son, who shed for us his blood,
Who, with the Holy Ghost, on high
Doth live and reign eternally. Amen.

Little Chapter.

But thou, O Lord, art among us, and thy holy name is invoked upon us, forsake us not, O Lord our God.

R. Thanks be to God.

V. Into thy hands, O Lord, I commend my spirit.

R. Thou hast redeemed us, O Lord, the God of truth.

Glory be to the Father, and to the Son, and to the Holy Ghost.

Into thy hands, O Lord, I commend my spirit.

V. Keep us, O Lord, as the apple of thine eye.

R. Protect us under the shadow of thy wings: save us.

Nunc dimittis, or the Song of Simeon.

1 Now dost thou dismiss thy servant, Lord, in peace: according to thy word:

2 For mine eyes have seen : thy salvation.

3 Which thou hast prepared : before the face of all people :

4 A light to enlighten the Gentiles: and the glory of thy people Israel.

Glory be to the Father, &c.

Ant. Save us, O Lord, when we are awake; and keep us while we sleep: that we may watch with Christ, and rest in peace.

Lord have mercy on us.
Our Father.
I believe in God.

Let us pray.

Visit, we beseech thee, O Lord, this habitation, and drive far from it all snares

VESPERS.

of the enemy: let thy holy angels dwell herein, to preserve us in peace: and may thy blessing be always upon us. Through our Lord, &c.

V. The Lord be with you.
R. And with thy spirit.
V. Let us bless the Lord.
R. Thanks be to God.

The Blessing.

May the almighty and merciful Lord, Father, Son, and Holy Ghost, bless and preserve us.

R. Amen.

Antiphons of the Blessed Virgin.

Mother of Christ! hear thou thy people's cry,
Star of the deep, and Portal of the sky!
Mother of him who thee from nothing made,
Sinking we strive, and call to thee for aid:
Oh, by that joy which Gabriel brought to thee,
Thou Virgin first and last, let us thy mercy see.

V. The angel of the Lord announced unto Mary.
R. And she conceived of the Holy Ghost.

Let us pray.

Pour forth, we beseech thee, O Lord, thy grace into our hearts; that we, to whom the incarnation of Christ thy Son was made known by the message of an angel, may, by his passion and cross, be brought to the glory of his resurrection. Through the same Christ our Lord.

R. Amen.

Let us pray.

O God, who, by the fruitful virginity of Blessed Mary, hast given to mankind the rewards of eternal salvation; grant, we beseech thee, that we may experience her intercession for us, through whom we have deserved to receive the Author of life, our Lord Jesus Christ, thy Son. Who liveth, &c.

R. Amen.

V. May the divine assistance remain always with us.

R. Amen.

Our Father (*secretly*).

Hail, O Queen of Heav'n enthroned!
Hail, by angels mistress own'd!
Root of Jesse, Gate of morn,
Whence the world's true Light was born.
Glorious Virgin, joy to thee,
Loveliest whom in heaven they see.

Fairest thou where all are fair!
Plead with Christ our sins to spare.

V. Vouchsafe that I may praise thee, O sacred Virgin.

R. Give me strength against thine enemies.

Let us pray.

Grant, O merciful God, support to our frailty; that we who commemorate the holy Mother of God, may, by the help of her intercession, arise from our iniquities. Through the same Christ our Lord, &c.

R. Amen.

V. May the divine assistance remain always with us.

R. Amen.

Joy to thee, O Queen of Heaven! alleluia.
He whom thou wast meet to bear; alleluia.
As he promised, hath arisen; alleluia.
Pour for us to him thy prayer; alleluia.

V. Rejoice and be glad, O Virgin Mary; alleluia.

R. For the Lord hath risen indeed; alleluia.

Let us pray.

O God, who didst vouchsafe to give joy to the world through the resurrection of thy Son, our Lord Jesus Christ; grant, we beseech thee, that, through his Mother, the Virgin Mary, we may obtain the joys of everlasting life. Through the same Christ, &c.

R. Amen.

V. May the divine assistance remain always with us.

R. Amen.

Hail, holy Queen, Mother of mercy;
Our life, our sweetness, and our hope, all hail.
To thee we cry, poor banished sons of Eve;
To thee we sigh, weeping and mourning in this vale of tears.
Therefore, O our Advocate,
Turn thou on us those merciful eyes of thine;
And after this our exile, show us
Jesus, the blessed fruit of thy womb,
O merciful, O kind, O sweet Virgin Mary.

V. Pray for us, O holy Mother of God.

R. That we may be made worthy of the promises of Christ.

Let us pray.

Almighty, everlasting God, who, by the co-operation of the Holy Ghost, didst prepare the body and soul of Mary, glorious Virgin and Mother, to become the worthy habitation of thy Son ; grant that we may be delivered from instant evils and from everlasting death by her gracious intercession, in whose commemoration we rejoice. Through the same Christ, &c.

R. Amen.

V. May the divine assistance remain always with us.

R. Amen.

Prayer after Compline.

O blessed St. Michael and all ye holy angels of the Lord, defend us in the day of battle by your heavenly prayers, that so we perish not in the dreadful judgment; and ye most specially, our guardian angels, intercede for us to our Lord, that in all our thoughts, words, and deeds, we may be kept free from sin, and found pleasing in the sight of God.   Amen.

Before going to sleep, say:

The angel of the Lord encampeth around them that fear him.   Alleluia.

I say unto you that their angels do ever

behold the face of my Father who is in heaven. Alleluia.

Pray for us, O ye heavenly hosts, that we may be worthy of the promises of Christ.

THE END.

www.ingramcontent.com/pod-product-compliance
Lightning Source LLC
Chambersburg PA
CBHW031419160426
43196CB00008B/993